It's Up to You

Other books by Karen Casey

Each Day a New Beginning

Each Day a Renewed Beginning

Each Day a New Beginning: Journal

Change Your Mind and Your Life Will Follow

Let Go Now

Codepenence and the Power of Detachment

52 Ways to Live the Course in Miracles

Living Long, Living Passionately

All We Have Is All We Need

Peace a Day At a Time

The Language of Healing

20 Things I Know for Sure

The Good Stuff from Growing Up in a Dysfunctional Family

Getting Unstuck

My Story to Yours

Cultivating Hope

Be Who You Wanna Be

Serenity

The Miracle of Sponsorship

The Promise of a New Day

Fearless Relationships

Girls Only

Girl to Girl

A Boy's Book of Daily Thoughts

Daily Meditations for Practicing the Course

Keepers of the Wisdom: Reflections from Lives Well Lived

A Woman's Spirit: More Meditations for Women

A Life of My Own: Meditations on Hope and Acceptance

In God's Care: Daily Meditations on Spirituality in Recovery

If Only I Could Quit: Recovering from Nicotine Addiction

Worthy of Love

It's Up to You

A Practice to Change Your Life by Changing Your Mind

Karen Casey

Conari
Press

CORAL GABLES

Cover Design: Katia Mena
Cover Photo/illustration: stock.adobe.com
Layout & Design: Elina Diaz

For permission requests, please contact the publisher at:
Mango Publishing Group
2850 S Douglas Road, 2nd Floor
Coral Gables, FL 33134 USA
info@mango.bz

For special orders, quantity sales, course adoptions and corporate sales, please email the publisher at sales@mango.bz. For trade and wholesale sales, please contact Ingram Publisher Services at customer.service@ingramcontent.com or +1.800.509.4887.

It's Up to You: A Practice to Change Your Life by Changing Your Mind

Library of Congress Cataloging-in-Publication number: 2023934054
ISBN: (pb) 978-1-64250-975-5 (hc) 978-1-68481-297-4 (e) 978-1-64250-976-2
BISAC category code: PHI005000, PHILOSOPHY / Ethics & Moral Philosophy

I dedicate this book to all the women and men who have traveled the spiritual road with me. Together we are making a difference.

Also to my husband, Joe Casey, who is a wonderful spiritual partner, a great supporter in every way, and able to make my path easier every day of my life. I love this journey we are sharing. Thank you, Joe.

Table of Contents

Introduction 11

Week 1: **Tend Your Own Garden** 13

Week 2: **Seek Solutions** 29

Week 3: **Let Go of Outcomes** 45

Week 4: **Change Your Mind** 61

Week 5: **Choose to Act Rather Than React** 77

Week 6: **Give Up Your Judgments** 93

Week 7: **Remember That You Are Not in Control** 109

Week 8: **Discover Your Own Lessons** 125

Week 9: **Do No Harm** 141

Week 10: **Quiet Your Mind** 157

Week 11: **Every Encounter Is a Holy Encounter—Respond Accordingly** 173

Week 12: **Choose the Quiet Voice of Loving-Kindness** 189

Closing Thoughts 205

About the Author 207

Introduction

Welcome to *It's Up to You*, the companion book to *Change Your Mind and Your Life Will Follow*. *It's Up to You* grew out of discussions with a number of people about how to take the ideas presented in *Change Your Mind* and apply them, incrementally, a week at a time. There are twelve weeks' worth of messages, two for each day of the week—one for the morning and one to close the day—based on the specific principles contained in each of the twelve chapters.

My own journey in Twelve Step rooms has taught me that all change is incremental. I have also learned that the willingness to change is the necessary first step anyone must take, or nothing changes at all. No one turns to a book like this one, or its companion book, unless they have felt blocked by old behavior patterns. The good news is, you have already shown your willingness to try something different.

I am convinced because of the miracles that have happened in my own life that miracles will happen for you too. The shift in our way of thinking, a shift that makes everything more joyful and peaceful, can't be avoided when we begin to apply the principles contained in this little book. Even applying one principle occasionally benefits us in ways we'd not imagined possible.

When taken one day at a time, one week at a time, life will become different. It will be more manageable, more productive, more purposeful. It will be more hopeful. And it will be more peaceful. That's a promise I can safely make.

Now it's time to begin. You may want to keep a notebook or journal to record your thoughts about the daily messages. Enjoy every step of the way. This is a journey you will treasure because of its simplicity, and it's one that will affect you for the rest of your life.

Week 1
Tend Your Own Garden

The first week of meditations, coupled with assignments, are written to help you keep your focus where it belongs: on yourself! We are not privy to anyone else's divine plan. We generally see our own only in hindsight. But we can cultivate the willingness to trust that we are in God's care and that our work is very specific. And so is everyone else's.

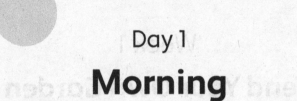

Day 1
Morning

Having anyone else as the focus of our attention will prevent us from doing the work that is ours to do.

It's so easy to sit in judgment of others, silently (or sometimes even audibly) criticizing them for their actions. Remembering that every person alive has a specific journey that includes a legion of activities has a way of eluding us. It's only our activities that deserve our attention.

We can learn from others, and that's why we share the path with so many. But we are not here to serve as judges; rather, we are here to be expressions of love.

I will literally count the number of times I reach out with love today and will write them down at the end of the day.

Day 1

Evening

Am I feeling good as I turn in for the night? Did I express my love for others by my actions? I will take a moment to remember the details of my day. Whom did I treat with kindness? Let me name them. Did they feel my expression of kindness? How could I tell?

Who didn't get my better self in our interactions? If I could redo these exchanges, what would I do differently? Do I owe any amends? If I do, I will make them tomorrow.

Day 2
Morning

Our attempts to control others are futile.

Wanting to control someone else usually grows out of our personal need to feel more secure. If "they"—whoever they might be—would only fulfill our will, it means they love us or honor us or accept our "superiority," thus making us worthy. How absurd, our attempt to control. How destructive this thinking is.

For today, let's remember that our security and worthiness come from our Higher Power, not someone else's behavior. Ever.

If someone does what I am hoping they will do today, it's because that person has chosen that action. Will I be able to see this idea revealed today? Taking time to write down an example will help me remember what to look for.

Day 2
Evening

As I reflect on the day, do I feel good about letting go of what others were doing? It's not easy, but it is possible. Every time I let a friend or stranger do something their way, I was relieved of a burden. Their success or failure wasn't tied to me in any way.

How many burdens did I let go of today? Can I name them? Every time I let go, my life was made more peaceful.

As I turn in for the night, I will thank my Higher Power for helping me let others be themselves today.

Day 3

Morning

Everyone we meet reveals something about ourselves.

Everyone on our path is divinely appointed. No one is present by accident. And how we choose to see each person is determined by the level of fear or love we are feeling in the moment. Our perception reveals our strengths, but also those traits that need correcting in ourselves.

Each person is a mirror of who I am. Making the decision to see as God would have me see is the assignment. Today will present many opportunities to see people as God would have me see them. I will savor and remember those times I fulfilled God's will by writing them down.

Day 3
Evening

What did I learn about myself today? How I saw others on my path will supply the information I now seek. Am I pleased with who I was in most encounters? I'll list some examples. Which areas of my behavior need addressing? Naming them will keep me honest. Did fear rule me in any situation today? I will re-"vision" that situation for a few moments before going to sleep tonight.

Having God as my companion in all situations means I always have a guide whose suggestions are impeccable. I have the capacity to follow God's lead. I know which voice is holy.

Day 4

Morning

Learning and then practicing new behaviors regarding our relationships with others can be exciting and very hopeful.

Any struggle we may be having at work or at home requires that we do something differently. We may not be totally at fault, of course, but we cannot change someone else's behavior or way of thinking. Fortunately, we can change our own.

That's the good news. It takes away a burden we don't need. Taking even a moment before responding to someone else's drama can change everything about the experience.

An idea as simple as gently smiling at everyone before even saying a word can make the day far more productive and peaceful, and far less dramatic. I will do this today and follow up by writing about the experiences I had.

Day 4
Evening

Did I do anything I felt proud of in my most significant relationship today? Let me name that. Was it difficult to "show up" differently? How did my behavior look in all other encounters? Writing an example will help me change it tomorrow. If I had the chance to repeat today, what's the first thing I could do that would make a difference?

Day 5
Morning

Freedom from the obsession of trying to control others releases one's spirit.

Keeping our attention on others limits our own personal growth. We miss what we have been born to do when we fail to pay heed to our own journey. Whatever someone on our path is doing might well be edifying; it may absorb us, but their presence isn't meant to be the whole substance of our development. Someone else can't be the center of our life, or we are being held hostage.

Being attentive to fellow travelers is courteous and part of the work we are here to do—their presence is intentional, after all. But being overly focused on them or, worse yet, trying to control them, isn't.

Day 5

Evening

Was today a good day? Was my life consumed at any time by my obsession with what someone else was doing? If it was, how could I have behaved instead? I will take a moment to reflect on this. I will write a note reminding myself of what I could do the next time I am allowing myself to be held hostage by another's behavior.

Day 6
Morning

It's an illusion to think we can control anyone else. Even our children have their own journeys.

It's easy to give up our attempts to control the people on our path. The neighbor's children or a friend's spouse may drive us mad, but we can accept our limitations pretty easily. But the closer to home others are, the stronger the desire to control them. Isn't their behavior a reflection on us, after all?

It's clear that I need to relinquish all control, even over my loved ones, today. I can make my wishes known. Period.

Day 6
Evening

Sharing with God or a loved one or friend the anguish, as well as the joys, of giving up control will free me from the need to think any more about this day that is passing. Each day is a new beginning, and tomorrow will give me practice sessions galore.

Day 7

Morning

We have so many more hours a day to appreciate the beauty all around us when we remember that we are not here to make hostages of others.

We will not walk this way again. That's a familiar phrase to all of us. But when we try to "tend another's garden instead of our own," we miss the beauty and the circumstances that have been prepared for us. While it's true that the people present have been gathered for a reason, they are not present to serve as our puppets—rather, as our teachers.

Day 7
Evening

Did I make the right choices today when considering the actions of others? Remembering that my friends and colleagues (along with my family of origin) are present to complement my life—not be its focus—clarifies my role.

Week 2
Seek Solutions

Week 2 will help you remember that obsessing about any problem exaggerates it. It doesn't resolve it. Resolution generally comes when we put our attention elsewhere, on helping others perhaps. When we give our Higher Power time to nudge us in the direction we need to go, resolution reveals itself to us.

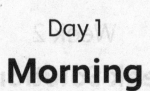

Day 1
Morning

Others watch how we behave. Does our behavior match what we say? Or are we making problems bigger than they are?

Alcoholics Anonymous suggests that attraction to its program is more effective than promotion of it. The same holds true for relationships, doesn't it? Telling others what they should do in regard to a problem will never be as effective as saying what has worked for us, or showing by our actions what is working now.

We can't change others. We can't control opinions, behaviors, how others see their problems or their dreams. We can only live our lives honestly, lovingly, openly, and hope that stands for something.

Day 1
Evening

Keeping our problems "right-sized" isn't always easy. How did I do today? Better yet, did I get a glimmer of understanding that there are really no problems in my life—only opportunities?

Day 2
Morning

Freeing others to handle their own problems makes us grateful for extended periods of peace. Being vigilant is the only requirement.

Hungering for peaceful lives comes with maturity, perhaps. But it remains elusive unless we make it our intention. There are myriad approaches to discovering peace. Meditation works for many. So does prayer, of course. The simple phrase, "I can see peace instead of this," can serve as a mantra too.

But one of the easiest ways to enjoy greater peace is by making the choice to let other people walk their own paths rather than engaging in their problems.

Day 2
Evening

Did I destroy my peace today by overreacting to a situation? Making a note of it will be a great reminder to avoid that behavior tomorrow.

Day 3

Morning

"Dancing" around the lives of others means missing our own. Is this our pattern? We can change it immediately if it is.

Making the decision to let others dance their own dance, experience their own problems, seek their own solutions, not trying to lead them or even follow them, is a thrilling and empowering experience of letting go that we all deserve. In fact, we will see quickly that we were not living life at all whenever someone else was in the center of our minds, particularly when that someone else triggered us to react rather than peacefully act.

Day 3
Evening

Being the center of my own life isn't the same as being self-absorbed. It simply means I have my attention where it belongs—on my goals and not on the goals or the problems of others.

Is there evidence that I lived this principle today? Were there times I passed up the opportunity to live it? How might I plan better for tomorrow?

Day 4
Morning

Letting go of others, loved ones or strangers, doesn't mean not caring.

On the contrary, letting go means we care a great deal. We want them to fully enjoy their successes and learn the lessons that wear their name. If we are overly involved in other people's lives, they won't be able to discern exactly what they accomplished themselves.

Relinquishing others to their own lives, making the choice to do nothing, even if challenged, isn't easy. But it is necessary, and it will let us be who we are meant to be too.

Day 4
Evening

I need constant reminders to let go. No one is in my life by chance; however, no one is in my life to be controlled either. Their behavior need not challenge me. It's my decision to back away and be peaceful. It's also my decision to be a good student as well as teacher.

Day 5

Morning

Trying to be the center of someone else's life will kill one's spirit.

Being in a relationship with others is good. Healing the human spirit depends on it. But choosing to be held hostage in any relationship means we have given up our identity and our connection to God. In making the relationship partner—be it a spouse, a friend, or a boss—our Higher Power, they become the one who defines us. When that happens, and it does all too often, inner chaos reigns, and neither party in the relationship can grow.

Day 5
Evening

Was I able to be both independent and interdependent today? Since the two perspectives complement each other, it's helpful to note when my behavior is illustrating one or the other. And as long as it's in line with one or the other, I am not being "dependent," which will hinder my personal growth and the growth of my companion too.

Dependence will not allow for healing to occur.

Day 6
Morning

Interdependence is the hallmark of a healthy relationship.

Getting enmeshed in someone else's life generally happens when we are feeling insecure. We cling and then mistakenly think that if we are constantly "in sync," we're meant for each other. The converse is the truth, of course. Dependence is never love, and it is never a sign of a healthy alliance. In fact, it screams unholy attachment to all onlookers.

Wanting healthy relationships takes a commitment to self-exploration and respect for our partner too. Knowing who we are and what we really want for ourselves is mandatory. Only then can we be a good partner and stay whole.

Day 6
Evening

Taking care of myself never means discounting the desires of my partner. However, how I express my needs is important to the healthy, peaceful flow of any relationship.

Day 7

Morning

Our own well-being is always the result of healthy decisions for ourselves coupled with disengagement from the choices of others.

Every one of us is responsible for our individual choices. Relying on God as the source for personal guidance has to be done by each of us too. For many, it's a major shift in perspective to claim responsibility for our choices, but it is empowering. Our lives will never be the same when we truly appreciate the depth of this responsibility and the freedom from chaos that it offers.

Day 7
Evening

Did I contribute to chaos today? Inner chaos can be just as immobilizing as stirring it up among my acquaintances. The voice I chose to hear today was reflected in the experiences I had. Those that were peaceful were under the guidance of God. Those that were chaotic had the ego as the architect.

Making a list of what experiences fall into each group will help me see what I want more of.

Week 3
Let Go of Outcomes

Week 3 will guide you every day to remember that God is always in charge of the outcome in every circumstance. Our job is limited; it's attention to the details in the effort we need to make. Nothing more. Some outcomes might match our hopes, but only when they also match God's will.

Day 1
Morning

Just because God is in charge doesn't mean we have nothing to do. On the contrary.

What is on the agenda every day? Many things—listening for God's will being one of them. Making the decision to hurt no one is another.

Paying attention to the people who are close by, thinking loving thoughts about them, and perhaps saying a prayer for them are activities we can do that will benefit all of humankind. And detaching from outcomes is perhaps our primary work every day.

Having God in charge doesn't relieve us of the responsibility to do our best to make this a better world. We are God's emissaries, after all. But being too focused on outcomes is not what God is looking for. At the end of the day, it's about effort, not outcome.

Day 1
Evening

Were my efforts loving and freely given today? It's never easy to detach from outcomes, but if they were my focus, I overstepped my boundaries with God and others.

Day 2
Morning

Our perceived problems have only the power and reality we give them.

Whatever we obsess about increases in magnitude. But removing our focus from a situation that we perceive as a problem lessens its importance and its impact.

Changing our focus, a decision available to all of us, can alter any experience. It can modify how we see any person. It can also temper any expectation.

In other words, our lives change as we take control of our minds, keeping them focused on our efforts rather than allowing ourselves to feel victimized by our situation.

Day 2
Evening

Am I willing to give up my so-called problems and choose instead to keep my focus limited just to what I can do right now, letting God guide the rest of what I might do later?

Day 3

Morning

Ordinary situations become big deals when we exaggerate them by trying to force an outcome that satisfies us.

Overreacting to the ordinary situation happens so naturally. Our self-centeredness and attachment to a particular outcome cause this tendency. The person in line ahead of us is taking too much time at the checkout, for instance. Don't they see all of us who are standing behind them?

Getting tied up in traffic or receiving a phone call at an inconvenient time can trigger a reaction that benefits no one if we have forgotten to be grateful that we can still drive a car and that people care enough to call us.

All situations are offering us opportunities to make loving efforts, nothing more.

Day 3
Evening

Were my efforts on behalf of myself and others kind or ill-conceived today? How many times did I try to control the outcome of a situation? Am I being honest with myself as I take an inventory of today's interactions?

Day 4
Morning

Unless our lives are in jeopardy, no situation has to upset us.

Making the choice to accept our experiences as they present themselves gets easier the more we practice this option. In fact, acceptance of even those situations we determine as unacceptable initially allows us to experience the serenity we deserve. Constant, or even occasional, discontent is never helpful. We don't know to where we are being guided.

We are not present in this world to be upset by our journey, or to upset the journey of anyone else. We are here with our chosen companions as way-showers and supporters. We are here to both teach and learn the next series of lessons we have been readied for. We are here to put forth the best effort we can, leaving every outcome to God.

Day 4
Evening

Freedom from upset is such a gift, and it's available to all of us when we remember to limit our focus to our efforts and not God's outcomes. That, coupled with my willingness to see as God would have me see, will make every situation easier to handle.

Day 5

Morning

Including God in every moment of our day changes how every experience appears.

We either believe in the presence of God or we don't. There is no in between. And making the choice to believe in God's presence, right now, makes every circumstance easier to walk through. For instance, if we get a pink slip at work, we may more easily believe that God is closing one door so another one can open. Or if our relationship partner chooses to leave us, we can remember that G od never takes from us whatever or whomever is right for us.

Acknowledging God throughout the day changes how we see every situation. It softens our perspective. It makes us want to express love, and it removes all fear from our minds and hearts.

Day 5
Evening

Was my day free from fear? Did I let God be my primary "learning partner"? I know that when I do this, I am at peace. Enumerating the many peaceful experiences I had today will show me how willing I was to let God "go before me."

Day 6

Morning

Overreacting to any situation is a sign we have forgotten to allow for God's guidance.

We all know how threatened we feel when someone overreacts to something we've said. We dig in, or worse. Seldom do we remember, in that moment, that the other person has forgotten God and may simply be afraid. Instead, we become afraid and lash out too.

But there is another way to respond to these situations. We can pause. We can take a deep breath. We can repeat the phrase, "I can see peace instead of this." And we can wait for God to show us the lesson behind the experience. There is always a lesson.

Day 6
Evening

Was fear present in my life today? Am I aware that I shortchanged God and the role he should have played? I also had other responses I could have made too. Now is a good time to replay those experiences in my mind, making the right responses this time.

Day 7
Morning

Remaining calm and cultivating joy can generally help defuse any tense situation.

Depending on the situation, we may need to remove ourselves. But that can be done quietly. Heaping verbal abuse on a tense situation only escalates the potential for a host of unnecessary repercussions.

It's important to remember that every situation can be seen more clearly through eyes that are warmed by the heart. It is our purpose to bring more peace and joy into all situations. Making the decision to ask the question "Am I bringing my better self into this moment?" has the potential for changing each experience and everyone present.

Day 7

Evening

Joy is a decision. Being calm is a decision. How many times today did I choose these responses? Did my choices have an impact on how others felt?

Day 7

Evening

Week 4
Change Your Mind

Week 4 will help you take full responsibility for every single one of your thoughts. Only when you do can you be certain of changing your life in the ways you desire. No one forces our thoughts on us. We willingly select them. We must "choose again" if we want a different life.

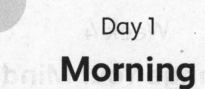

Day 1
Morning

There is a quiet voice within waiting to be heard.

There are two voices within. One is loud, argumentative, easily threatened, and quick to attack whomever is on the path. The other voice, our inner wisdom, is soft and seeks to respond to all experiences in a peaceful manner. Deciding which voice to listen to determines the life we will have.

We probably won't choose the peaceful voice in every instance, but choosing it even occasionally will have a beneficial effect on the people we walk among. And in turn, it will help them make a similar choice when an opportunity presents itself.

Day 1
Evening

Can I see how my choice to listen to one voice or the other influenced the day I experienced? It is the deciding factor, and letting this knowledge guide me empowers me to make the wiser of two choices, at least part of the time.

Keeping track of the results of my choices will remind me to make the "better one" more often.

Day 2
Morning

Retaliation, even when attacked, is never necessary.

Walking away from an ugly situation might never have occurred to us, but it's possible and it becomes easier with practice. Just knowing we don't have to engage in every argument we've been invited to, that we don't have to participate in every fight that is happening in our midst, is like being released from prison.

Old ideas can, and often do, hold us hostage. But we can free ourselves. It's a small decision that gets made over and over again. One day at a time. One experience at a time.

Day 2
Evening

Did I refrain from being mean, or worse, when someone attacked me today? Did I remember that anyone's attack is really about their fear and doesn't have anything to do with me? It's not easy to remember this, but with practice, we can grow in our understanding of this principle. Fearful people find it hard to be kind and accepting.

Day 3

Morning

When others attack us, they are generally afraid.

What an eye-opener this idea is to many of us. I grew up thinking bullies were tough and to be avoided at all costs. When I experienced rage in my family, I had no clue it was covering up fear. Knowing it now doesn't lessen the angst it might cause, but it does explain the dynamic in a way that makes it understandable, even forgivable when we are ready.

Making the decision to see the inner spirit of the attacker rather than the attack itself is a practice that can be honed. When we do this, we help the attacker make a better choice the next time too. Seeing only as God would see is the assignment, after all. It's not easy, but it is possible.

Day 3

Evening

Was I the attacker today or the one attacked? Regardless of which it was, I know fear was the instigator. Attack is seldom physical. More often, it's a verbal put-down or even a look of disapproval or disgust. However I was a party to any of these forms today, I will note them. Denying their presence helps none of us.

Day 4

Morning

Making the choice to do nothing in the face of an angry attack is calming to all who are present. First comes the thought.

Gently smiling or saying a silent prayer during a tense moment with another person is soothing. We don't have to let our emotions add fuel to any situation.

We are always being given opportunities to show others there is another way to see, feel, think, and live. Even the most intense and alarming circumstance can be perceived as an opportunity for calm if we are willing to be the example.

Day 4
Evening

I was responsible for any thought I had today. No other person was to blame. If my thoughts were negative toward a person or a situation, I added chaos to the experience we all share in this life. I can take charge of my thinking in a more positive way tomorrow. That's the good news. None of today's situations have to become tomorrow's baggage.

Day 5

Morning

We have to be willing to change how we think if we want different experiences in our lives. Understanding that our willingness is the first step should be a simple undertaking, but it seldom is.

Becoming willing is an action. It's a definite change in our state of mind. It doesn't happen of its own accord. When we understand this and seek to become willing, the God of our understanding will show up, and willingness will be our gift.

It's not easy to accept responsibility for all that has occurred in our lives. But had we thought differently about the circumstances, the results would have been different.

Day 5
Evening

Was I peaceful or agitated today? Am I able to see how my thoughts determined my experiences? Was there a time I became willing to begin again when my thoughts hooked me into behavior that I didn't really like? Answering these questions will help chart my course for tomorrow.

Day 6

Morning

Don't let any thought hold you hostage.

If our thoughts are not comforting us, we can change them. What a concept! If they are creating anxiety in us or pushing us to be either argumentative or withdrawn, we have the capacity to think another thought—one that's helpful or loving, or one that engages others in a positive way—thus changing our experience in that moment.

If we are being held hostage by thoughts that fit a past reality, we have only ourselves to blame. The only moment that matters is the one we are presently experiencing. No thought has the power to control our actions now. And no thought happens without our acquiescence.

Day 6
Evening

As I review my experiences today, am I pleased? That's the important question. What, specifically, pleased me? What thoughts did I need to discard? What can I watch for in the future regarding my thoughts? Making some notes will help me remember the "better way of thinking" tomorrow.

I probably have a "default" button. Most of us do. That's the one I push when I am too lazy to choose a more productive or loving thought.

Day 7

Morning

Thoughts create perception, and our perception has only the reality we give it.

Some believe that a miracle is a simple shift in perception, a choice available to any of us at any moment. How we see any situation is usually dependent on our past experiences coupled with the level of love or fear we are feeling in the moment.

In other words, we bring to every situation whatever meaning it has for us. That's both the good news and the bad news. We can't blame others for anything, but we can see the glass as full every time.

Day 7

Evening

Did my day flow smoothly? If so, can I recognize what my part was and make a mental note of it? If I felt agitated, can I accept responsibility and make a new plan for the next time a similar experience occurs? Because it will! Now is a good time to sketch out this plan.

Week 5

Choose to Act Rather Than React

Week 5 will empower you to be who you want to be in every situation. Saying "I just can't help it" when you react to a situation that is irritating or out of your control simply isn't productive. Nor is it allowing you to grow into the person you have been born to be.

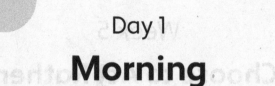

Day 1
Morning

Letting external stimuli decide who we are prevents our ever feeling grounded and whole.

Letting the negative looks or mean-spirited comments from others determine how we feel about ourselves is not only debilitating, it makes it impossible for us to offer the lessons the people sharing our path are seeking today. Everyone is present intentionally. We simply can't be who we are supposed to be if we have allowed others to define us.

Remembering to let the behavior of others roll off of us is a habit that can be cultivated. Even when someone's behavior is kind, we need to remember that it doesn't determine who we are. We determine who we are—period!

Day 1
Evening

Whether others were kind or dismissive today isn't what I need to remember now. Who was *I*? That's the significant question. Taking an inventory of the day's activities will reveal my strengths and my weaknesses. In turn, that reveals where I need to put my attention tomorrow.

Day 2

Morning

Every encounter offers us an opportunity to be who we want to be.

It is exciting to know that no one has the power to take charge of our thinking or our actions in any circumstance. Many of us, for far too long, gave our power willingly to others. It may have seemed easier than standing up for ourselves. Or maybe it was habitual. Or perhaps depression curtailed us. For sure, we simply didn't know how good empowerment would feel, or we would have been more assertive long ago.

Day 2
Evening

The empowerment I felt today was the direct result of how I presented myself in one circumstance after another. Not letting someone else decide who I would be felt good. I can make this choice habitual. It's a good habit too, a better one than many I have honed in the past.

Day 3

Morning

Being dependent on the opinions of others keeps us stuck and small-minded. It also edges out God.

On our path are many people, most of them as self-absorbed as we tend to be. However, we are the teachers and the students, interchangeably, who have been called to participate with one another in each moment. What we hear and what we say, if we have relied on God as the interpreter, are the messages that are needed by all of us.

Inviting God into each moment will allow us to hear and speak the "holy words" that all of us are ready for.

Day 3
Evening

Was my day peaceful? Or did I let the egos of others control my thoughts? I have the power every moment to choose whom to be dependent on: God, my ego, or the opinions of others. My peace is guaranteed when I make the right choice. I can see this.

Day 4
Morning

A knee-jerk reaction to any situation or person will likely not lead to the peaceful encounter that is destined to take us to the next right experience on our divine path.

Many of today's experiences will trigger anger, sullenness, or hurt feelings. But taking a deep breath before making any comment or taking any action will allow us a moment to switch gears. All it takes is a moment to get a new perspective.

Practicing this technique gives us a new way to experience our lives. It heals more than our relationships too. Deep breathing brings healing to our bodies as well.

Day 4

Evening

Did taking a deep breath or pausing for just a moment save me from some ugly encounters today? That was the purpose of today's suggestion. If I didn't succeed every time, that's okay. Just trying to live more purposefully and consciously counts. My effort is noted by God.

Day 5

Morning

Detaching from the turmoil in the lives of our companions is never easy but always necessary.

We are easily seduced into thinking that it's our job to help others resolve their problems or respond to the conflicts confronting them. Our egos want to be engaged. Our egos want to control the details in all too many lives. But our egos will never help anyone, not even ourselves.

Everyone has their lessons to experience. If we get into problem-solving for others, we prevent the learning that needs to happen for them.

Day 5

Evening

How well did I do today? Can I see how my interference with the experiences of others complicated matters? Demonstrating detachment from the insanity in others' lives enhances peace in my own life, and that is the best example I can set for anyone. Did I see evidence of this today?

Day 6
Morning

Blaming others for what has happened, is happening, or might happen in our lives will never allow us to contribute the good that is ours to give.

The inclination to blame others for every situation that makes us unhappy is so strong. We were probably trained by our parents to do this. It's the human condition to shirk responsibility for what we are experiencing (unless it's good, of course). But the willingness to be accountable for everything that is happening empowers us to change the parts of our lives we aren't happy with. We can't do it any other way.

Day 6
Evening

Did I blame someone else for anything that happened to me today? If so, I owe them amends, and I will make a note of that so I don't forget to do it. My work here is to be responsible for myself and to do God's will. When I blame others, I am doing neither.

Day 7

Morning

The mood swings of others have nothing to do with us. What a difficult realization this is for many. If insecurity plagued us during childhood, it may shadow us still on occasion, in which case, the natural response to someone else's outburst might be to cower or to assume responsibility for it.

It's not just the anger of others that might influence how we feel. Their happiness, too, might secure our own, for a moment. This is just as foolhardy.

What others do or say or feel simply does not have the power to control how we feel or think or act unless we relinquish these to them. How sad if we do—how unfulfilled our lives will be.

Day 7
Evening

How many mood swings did I avoid getting trapped by today? Keeping track of them will help me practice this exercise tomorrow too. Learning new techniques for living more peacefully is what prepares me to demonstrate better living for others too.

Week 6

Give Up Your Judgments

Loving others and judging others are mutually exclusive. And we are doing one or the other, perhaps unconsciously, but nonetheless constantly. Our judgments prevent us from grasping the lesson in the moment. They also keep us separate. Only when we are joined can we heal the inner wounds that are common to all of us.

Judgments reveal who we are, not who someone else is. That simply doesn't feel good, not for long anyway. The solution is gratitude. It can be practiced anytime, anyplace. Throughout Week 6, we will get lots of practice.

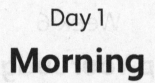

Day 1
Morning

Developing the attitude of unconditional love is a decision, followed by daily, even moment-by-moment, practice.

Unconditional love is not easy. Having conditions placed on us when we were young, perhaps by parents and teachers, taught us to do likewise with others. But God doesn't place conditions on us, so we have a pattern to follow. We can best begin the practice by developing the willingness to be grateful for every person who walks the path with us. They are divinely present as our opportunities to express the love of God.

Loving without conditions makes each experience easier, really. There is no guesswork involved. No "they should have" or "if they'd only" to help us decide our next action. What we do next is simply love the person whether we love their behavior or not.

Day 1
Evening

Being loving is an action step. Did I take this step as often as I could have today? When I withheld my love, how did it feel? Can I see what triggered my willingness to love and what triggered my resistance to it? By writing a brief narrative about how the day went, I will see more clearly the changes I can make tomorrow.

Day 2

Morning

Judgments create a feeling of separation from others. We can't heal ourselves or help others heal in this state.

Our feelings of separation grow out of our insecurity and then in turn heighten it. It becomes a vicious cycle. But there is a remedy: reach out to others with sincere appreciation for their presence. Fear doesn't have to rule our behavior. It may still be present, but it diminishes in size every time we offer an expression of love or acceptance to a fellow traveler.

Being aware of our oneness with others is an acquired habit, one that warms us to the bone when we have experienced it fully. The more we honor this awareness, the less inclined we will be to judge others unkindly.

Day 2
Evening

Habits can be strengthened. They can also be broken. Which ones did I strengthen today? Did my behavior enhance the life of anyone else? Although it is not my responsibility to improve another person's life, how I treat someone else will have an effect on my own development too.

Day 3
Morning

Negative judgments about any one affect our relationships with everyone. What we feel toward one is felt by all—the good and the bad.

Fear is the root of all negative judgments. We simply can't doubt this principle. Fortunately, we can learn how to live without fear. It visits us when we forget that our Creator is as close as our breath; when we forget that all the people we walk among are divinely appointed to share our path; when we forget that we have a purpose and it's to love one another and be grateful.

We have a choice in every moment to express love or judgment. Either is a habit that can be honed.

Day 3

Evening

What's my score at the end of this day? Did I give the gift of love as often as possible? Or did I fall back on my old behavior of being judgmental?

It's not easy to make the more loving choice every time, particularly if fear has been a near-constant companion. If I make a list of all the encounters in which I did offer the hand of love and friendship, I will see that this new behavior can become the more practiced one.

Day 4

Morning

The practice of unconditional love can be viewed as an adventure. Whether or not we received it in our family of origin is irrelevant.

Expressing unconditional love doesn't come naturally to most of us. We are far more inclined to compare ourselves to others, feeling better or worse than them with each comparison. The end result is that we don't feel much joy. And we certainly don't spread much either.

Anticipating the expression of unconditional love like an adventure makes offering it as often as possible like a game where everyone wins. What a thoughtful way to contribute to the world around us!

Day 4

Evening

Is my scorecard today one I am proud of? It's not easy to be unconditionally loving, is it? Only God does it perfectly. Our parents seldom did. Even our dearest friends and partners find it hard. But we can try. That's all that's expected. That's what today's scorecard is for.

Day 5

Morning

Shifting from judgments that imprison us to seeing the good in others magnifies the good we will see and feel in all our relationships.

Shifting our perception so that we may see the good in the people who walk among us makes it easier to demonstrate this way of seeing to others. We are, after all, teachers as well as students. And it's a decision we make every time our gaze passes from one person to another. There is always good to be seen, the same good others see in us. Remember the phrase we have heard so often, "God doesn't make junk"?

Day 5
Evening

How many good qualities did I notice in my friends and associates today? Was I as conscious of them as I might have been? Making a list of all of them will help me stay committed to seeing them again tomorrow. I see that which I want to see. I think that which I want to think. I am not powerless over these things.

Day 6
Morning

We will never experience peace if we listen to the voice of the ego in our minds that constantly vies for our attention.

The ego never wants us to be joined in a loving way with others. It prefers that we feel separate, alone, fearful, and judgmental. But there is another voice within that we can listen to. It's the one belonging to our Higher Power. It never judges negatively, ourselves or anyone else. It always speaks softly and lovingly, and offers us gentle guidance for all of our questions.

It's our choice, in every instance, which voice we will listen to. Both are present. One leads to harmony in our lives and the world around us. The other one breeds havoc in our families, neighborhoods, and among countries too.

Day 6
Evening

Which voice was I the most attentive to today? My level of peace is a good indicator. How often was I agitated? Can I see how my willingness to listen to the wrong voice contributed to that? Making a chart of what happened and my behavior around it will give me good insight about today. It will give me a good blueprint for tomorrow too.

Day 7
Morning

Today, look at each relationship, each encounter, as if it's the only one you will ever have to act the way God wants you to act.

If we could look at each opportunity with another person from this perspective, everything about our lives would change forever. The expression of this level of love and acceptance would soften our inner core while softening the core of everyone else too.

What can make this a manageable idea is to realize that we don't ever have to look beyond the moment, the encounter, that's right before us. We don't have to anticipate the difficulty we might face later in the day. We can let God be with us and think for us in each moment, and our lives will change.

Day 7

Evening

Did I resist expressing God's love today? Can I see how that prevented me from feeling the joy I might have felt? Can I understand that I will get a similar opportunity to express my love tomorrow? Will I step up to the plate then?

Week 7

Remember That You Are Not in Control

The obsession to control others is strong. This generally grows out of the fear that if we let others live their own lives freely, they might choose to live them separate from us. In reality, unless we give up control, they will most likely seek separation from us.

But we can develop the willingness to give up control with our Higher Power's help. The freedom we will experience when we give up control is powerful, educational, and overwhelmingly peaceful. It fills us with the inspiration to go to new places in our own lives. Throughout Week 7, we will get to practice this.

Day 1

Morning

We will never attain peaceful lives if we are intent on controlling others.

Even our children have their own journeys to make, their own choices, their own mistakes, their own joys and sorrows. While we can offer suggestions and our own behavior can set a good example, we simply can't make our children do our will.

Letting them manage their own lives promises us such joy in time. However, we must experience this act of surrender in order to understand the truth of this principle. Once we have thoroughly enjoyed the fruits of letting them go, we will not so quickly return to our old behavior.

Day 1
Evening

Letting go was my big challenge today. How did I do? How many occasions were there when I quietly gave in to a situation, sought a new perspective, perhaps, or simply walked away rather than engage in a battle, one I might even have won?

Taking note of the many times I opted not to control is the real lesson of this day. It gets easier the more I practice it.

Day 2

Morning

The seduction of trying to control others results from our occasional successes.

When others do what we want them to do, we mistakenly pat ourselves on the back. We fail to see their choice as serving them but rather assume they are fulfilling our wishes. Others change when they want to. Period. And that's a blessing we don't quite understand until we have enjoyed the fruits of it.

Our desire to control others, particularly those we consider significant to our lives, is due to the threat we feel when they express opinions or plans that aren't consistent with ours. Our fear can only be quelled by remembering God in those moments. What others choose to do, even when it pleases us, can never offer the peace that God's love promises.

Day 2
Evening

Did I have a peaceful day? What made it so? What might I have done differently those times I lacked peace? Was my lack of peace due to my attempts to control someone else or a circumstance that wasn't mine to control?

Day 3

Morning

We are not the center of the universe, nor are we the center of anyone else's life.

When the truth of this sinks in, we realize how lucky we really are. Having every situation and every person revolve around us is a heavy burden to be saddled with. Our own lives get too little attention when our focus is "out there." Each one of us is here to complete specific work, and the work of any one of us does not include doing the work of someone else (or expecting them to do their work according to our specifications).

Because we are traveling this path with so many others, perhaps it's easy to confuse our separate but complementary journeys. Learning to appreciate the presence of one another is all we are really expected to do.

Day 3
Evening

Do I get any gold stars for the day? Or did I give in to the seduction of trying to control someone else's actions? It's not easy to stay on my side of the street, but when I remember that not letting you be in control of yourself hurts your growth, it becomes easier to back off.

The riches in my life are multiplied every time I keep my focus where it belongs.

Day 4
Morning

Being powerless over others is one of the best gifts we have been given on this journey.

Trying to manage the affairs of others is frustrating. In fact, it's hopeless. We make our own lives unmanageable when trying to manage the affairs of others. We can't fulfill the purpose that is ours if our attention is always on someone else.

If you are going to bed at night feeling either unfulfilled or very tired, it's most likely because you have spent the day trying to coax others to do your will. This is not your purpose here. Give up the struggle now. Change your mind now. Experience the peace now.

Day 4

Evening

Was my day misspent? In what way? What do I feel best about? If I could do one thing over today, what would it be? Can I see how I got off track? My life will never be perfect, but as long as I can see improvement, I have a chance to be all that I am meant to be.

Day 5

Morning

No one shows up in our life by accident.

This is a powerful idea, but not one that is easily accepted when the person standing before us is angry, shaming, or worse. We have requested our teachers and our lessons. We have simply forgotten that in the heat of the moment.

That no one wanders into our lives by accident doesn't mean we should tolerate unacceptable behavior—on the contrary. But it does mean that there is a lesson to be gleaned from each experience. And I have learned, again and again, that choosing to bypass the lesson "because it doesn't feel good" doesn't relieve me of the necessity to learn it at a later time. Our purpose will not be fulfilled without surrendering to all of our lessons. The time we do so is ours.

Day 5
Evening

Did someone new cross my path today? Was I prepared for whatever lesson ensued? Was there a conflict I might have avoided, or did I learn something that I can already see will benefit me? Can I see how the many people I have known throughout my life are part of the tapestry that is being woven? No one is without a part to play. Am I grateful for this?

This is the right time to share my thoughts on the people, the places, and the lessons. Is there a pattern to what I am seeing here?

Day 6

Morning

Not all lessons are life-changing. In fact, some are quite ordinary.

Remember when we were in school and our textbooks had review sections at the end of certain chapters? Some of life's lessons are like that. We get repeat opportunities to practice them because of their importance to the overall plan for our lives. Not every experience is a new lesson, but every experience fits comfortably into the bigger picture of our lives.

It's so refreshing to realize that absolutely nothing is happening that hasn't been factored into our divine plan. We are ready for whatever is happening, and we don't have to understand this for it to be true.

I am where I need to be, and I am ready for what is to come next. I am relieved to know this even in those moments that doubt sets in.

Day 6
Evening

Which lessons did I relish today? What specifically did they teach me? Were any of these lessons ones I had avoided previously? Am I able to see how my presence in someone else's life was necessary to a lesson that person was ready to learn? Writing a narrative covering all of these points will clarify the important things to remember about my life today.

Being willing to celebrate the many steps of my journey today will help me look forward to what's coming tomorrow.

Day 7
Morning

A concerted effort to control someone else might lead to such disharmony in the relationship that the inevitable split is irreparable.

If we remember that our journeys intersect with those people we need as our teachers, we might think twice before too forcefully pushing our opinions on them. It's simply not to anyone's advantage to insist that friends or strangers agree with us. Being right isn't the goal; being peaceful is.

In every instance we have to decide if we want harmony or agitation in our relationships. Once we have decided, then we must act accordingly. Letting other people live their own lives will lead to harmony. Nothing else can guarantee it.

I can foster peace wherever I go today by how I interact with friends and strangers. I chart the course.

Day 7

Evening

Was I an instrument for peace today? Making a list of those examples will serve as reminders for future days. Any success I had today can be repeated. Unfortunately, so can any failure. I will reframe the failures too, so I can see what the better choice in behavior might have been.

I am empowered by the good choices I made today. They are a great blueprint for tomorrow as well.

Week 8

Discover Your Own Lessons

Our primary lesson in life, and in Week 8, is to learn forgiveness. This, coupled with a willingness to express only love in every situation, is what allows us to know peace. Our interactions with others are the chances we have for grasping this primary lesson, and we must remain aware that our minds control every detail of every thought and every experience. If we don't like any part of "out there," we must go within and seek another perspective on the experience.

The fortuitous element here is that our mind is not and never has been an empty vessel with no purpose other than being filled up by the actions or thoughts of others. We choose what we focus on and then cultivate it in our minds. What others say and do are not irrelevant. There is no such thing as an irrelevant idea, in fact. Every one of them is offering us something. But we don't have to adopt as our own any idea or perspective that isn't conducive to our peace of mind.

Day 1
Morning

Having someone else's life on your mind doesn't allow you to absorb the more important experiences that are trying to get your attention now.

Codependency is the popular term that describes being focused on someone else at the expense of yourself. Specifically, it means valuing someone else's life more than your own. It might even mean excluding your own all together. No one is helped by this behavior, which for many becomes an obsession. No one is allowed to freely learn the lessons that are theirs to learn under these circumstances.

Our security doesn't come from how we are perceived by others, nor in how many others we "help" through our attention. Our security is guaranteed by our Higher Power. Having that relationship as the focus of our lives makes every experience a joy and clarifies our direction.

Paying attention to where my mind is today will make the difference between having a peaceful day and one that's unfocused and anxious.

Day 1
Evening

As I end the day, how would I evaluate the many experiences I had? Was I too intent on the life of someone else? If so, how did that affect my performance at work and with others? Did I let the actions of someone else determine my own? What could I have done differently? I will share what I learned so I can refrain from making this an ingrained habit.

I am hopeful that my codependency will lessen, one encounter at a time. I will share with someone an example of how I accomplished this today.

Day 2
Morning

Codependency is a mindset that has claimed the lives of millions of people.

Letting someone else's behavior, regardless of what it is, define who we are and how we behave never gives us any breathing room to grow into the people we are being called to be. Giving someone else the responsibility for how we behave is, at the very least, immature. It guarantees we will not fulfill the purpose for which we are here in a very timely fashion.

Allowing our lives to revolve, willy-nilly, around the lives of others keeps us stuck in their drama. When we live this way, we forget that we have a mission here, and it's not to live in the shadows of others—or to hold those others as hostages. We must be free and give others their freedom too if we are to know peace.

I have the capacity to be peaceful today, but do I have the willingness? Giving my attention to God, first, will begin a smooth journey.

Day 2
Evening

How smooth was my journey today? Was I impatient? Embarrassed? Ashamed? Did I struggle with how someone else was behaving? How many times did I let my feelings fall sway to another's mood or words? Writing a detailed narrative of who I was today based on who others around me were will illustrate the areas I need to work on. God is waiting to help.

I know that God wants me to fulfill my role. What's the first thing I will do tomorrow?

Day 3

Morning

Doing for someone else what they need to do for themselves keeps both of us stuck. We must be vigilant about minding our own business.

Developing healthy boundaries is a process that takes time, willingness, perseverance, and a clear understanding of their importance to each of us. Boundaries aren't meant to keep us separate, but to allow each of us to grow in our own way, at the rate that fits for us.

It became our habit, perhaps, to caretake as a way of remaining "necessary" to others. If we kept them dependent on us, our lives would have purpose. In that dynamic, our own lessons rush swiftly by, unnoticed, while we stay attached to our hostages. Fortunately, the lessons will make their appearance again, but our caretaking prevents the hostages from learning theirs too.

I will keep my focus where it belongs today: on me. This will benefit everyone else too.

Day 3
Evening

If I am not feeling peaceful tonight, the reason is clear: I was not keeping my attention where it belonged. If my sights are always on others, I'll be disappointed, feel ignored, or seem unappreciated.

Now is a good time to review my day. What will I do again tomorrow? What will I do differently? Being specific will make it easier to be committed to change.

Day 4

Morning

If we want to be good students of life, our minds must not be cluttered by thoughts of others.

We are not being asked to ignore the presence of others. On the contrary, others are always present because of the mutually beneficial lessons we offer and receive. But being obsessed by others' presence, capabilities, and even failings, prevents us from receiving the direction we need from our own lessons—direction that is only accessible in the quiet spaces of our minds.

Our lives are joined for a purpose. We are not alive to cultivate separate existences. But there is a difference between being good stewards of our own lives and being loving participants in the lives of our companions.

I will honor the participants in my life today, but I will not let thoughts of them be my only thoughts.

Day 4
Evening

Where was my attention today? Noticing the others sharing my journey is good, but not if it's at the expense of my own journey. How do I evaluate my day using that as a measure? Where can I do a better job of living my own life? Writing my thoughts down will be helpful when tomorrow comes.

I am noticing things about my way of living in this world that I hadn't noticed before. I will make a note of at least one of them.

Day 5

Morning

Being attuned to our inner voice takes concentration and willingness.

There are two inner voices, actually. One belongs to the ego, and it judges, attacks, and tells us we're worthless. It also pushes us to control people, places, and things, however foolhardy that suggestion may seem at the time. The other voice is loving and quiet, much harder to hear and definitely committed to our peace. We have to really *want* to hear it or we will miss its guidance. There is a way to tap into that voice, however. Begin counting your blessings. Every time we recount, for ourselves or someone else, something we're grateful for, we will become aware that God has always been present doing for us what we hadn't been able to do for ourselves.

I will give my attention to the quieter inner voice today. It assures me that God is close and all is well.

Day 5
Evening

Where was my attention today? On which voice? My experiences will certainly make that clear. Did I have a peaceful day? Was I willing to express kind words to others? Or was I eager to blame and pass judgment?

I'll make a list of the times I listened to the ego and those times I made the wiser choice. Which list is longer? What will I do tomorrow?

Day 6

Morning

Our minds are ours to control. Let's be grateful.

Claiming full responsibility for ourselves—every action, thought, hope, and plan—is empowering, a bit intimidating, and the right attitude to have if we want to fulfill the work we've been called here to do. It also allows little time to manage the actions, thoughts, hopes, and plans of our fellow travelers, to the benefit of all.

Because the society we live in has grown accustomed to blaming other people for every troubling circumstance, we learn to follow suit at an early age. But there is another way to move through life's experiences. And we can do it, starting right now. We can step back from each situation for a moment and review what part is ours to handle and what part our companions need to handle in order for them to fulfill their own purpose.

I can't be made to do anything I don't agree with today—nor can anyone else. I will remember to keep my focus where it belongs.

Day 6
Evening

At the end of the day, am I truly grateful that my mind is in my control? The downside is that I wasn't able to blame anyone else. Or if I did, I now need to make amends. Do I have any to make? This is the right time to list those people. This is also the right time to keep a tally of the times I accepted responsibility for my behavior.

Can I see where I need more work tomorrow?

Day 7

Morning

Depression is real for many people.

There are many reasons one of us might feel depressed. Perhaps a loved one has departed. Or we might have lost a job. Kids leaving home can trigger it for some parents. Myriad situations contribute to depression, and often it passes of its own accord.

Another contributor to depression—a big one in fact—is obsession with what others are doing or not doing. When our lives are consumed by someone else's life, we feel lost, afraid, and extremely unfulfilled. Losing sight of who we are and what our purpose is reduces us to a depression that is often tenacious. Medication is sometimes necessary, but the primary solution is to get our minds back on our lives, our work, our hopes and dreams.

I can cultivate a peaceful state of mind, if that's what I really want. Depression need not dog me today, or any day.

Day 7

Evening

My life reflected the contents of my mind today. Was it a good day?
What about it could have been better? What would a perfect day look
like? Writing that scenario will give me the structure to help it manifest
in one of my tomorrows.

I will remember that tomorrow will mirror whatever is uppermost
in my mind. Carrying into sleep the picture of how a good tomorrow
might look will help me experience it.

Week 9
Do No Harm

This suggestion needs no clarification. We are either being helpful or not, kind or not, loving or not.

Anything short of kindness, love, or helpfulness may not be intentionally harmful, but it still misses the mark.

Every instance of the coming week will give us multiple opportunities to show that we understand the difference between harming someone and letting that person know that they matter in our lives and in the lives of others too. Harm isn't necessarily physical. Disinterest can be also be interpreted as harm.

Choosing an expression of kindness is always the best choice. Let's devote Week 9 to constant practice.

Day 1

Morning

Watching what we say and how we say it is a good way to avoid the tendency to do harm to anyone.

Our words can be weapons—or they can help to heal wounds. We always know when we are being loving and when we are offering subtle or not-so-subtle put-downs. Making the choice to be anything but kind is the fault of the ego. However, *we're* in charge of the ego. We need to grasp the fact that whatever we put out there will come back tenfold. This goes for the good as well as the bad.

This principle takes the guesswork out of every interaction we have. If we aren't responding in a kind manner to the person who has just spoken to us, regardless of their words or manner, we are not fulfilling our part of God's plan for us.

Within each moment is my opportunity to show God and my companions that I understand the difference between healing and hurtful words.

Day 1
Evening

Do I feel good about how I spoke to my fellow travelers today? Was there any time that I cringed over what I said or how I said it? Seeing my failing here, and then admitting it to my companion, will help me remember the next time a similar situation comes up.

The choice to use kind words isn't that hard. The choice to use a gentle voice is easy too. I will be better prepared tomorrow.

I will spend a few moments envisioning this behavior, seeing me in the company of a companion, as I pass into sleep.

Day 2

Morning

Choosing the high road in our interactions with others will always serve us well.

We never have to treat someone unkindly just because they have treated us that way. Remember, our companions are the teachers we have sought to learn our next set of lessons from. And the primary lesson is to be kind, regardless of the person or circumstance. Only briefly are we gratified when we have been rude in response to another's rudeness. In that moment, our spirit is harmed just as much as the spirit of our companion.

Our feelings of insecurity lead to our being rude. Because we feel less than, we want to punish those close by, thus locking in our feelings of separateness. It's a vicious cycle, but it can be broken if we take a tiny step of kindness toward our companion.

I have a small assignment today, one that will transform any experience in a significant way: I will be kind in every encounter.

Day 2
Evening

Well, how was my day? What might have made it better? Was there any instance when I fell back into old behavior? Did something trigger that? Did I have any interaction that felt really good? What made it so? Is there something either large or small that I learned that can be applied again tomorrow? It will help me to journal about that. In fact, I will share responses to all of these questions.

I am so lucky to be choosing another way of seeing and acting. I know that my life is becoming better for it. Is there an obvious payoff that I can see already?

Day 3
Morning

Keeping our behavior kind one day at a time makes our life more manageable and far more peaceful.

We can do anything for a day, can't we? One of the slogans of Alcoholics Anonymous is "One day at a time." The first time I saw that placard on a wall, I scoffed. My whole life was being lived in the future. But after many years of a-day-at-a-time living, I am comforted knowing that I don't have to get lost in tomorrow or worry about what may never happen. Staying in this moment is quite peaceful, and it's all we're guaranteed.

Being loving is not always easy, is it? Some of the people who cross our path are mean-spirited, or worse. But making the effort to see them through the eyes of God will allow us to be loving. And for this one day, we can do it.

Do I have the willingness to stay in this day? It's all that's being asked—that along with being loving.

Day 3
Evening

What a relief to be living just one day at a time. I am comforted by this, aren't you? How did you do today? How many times did you get ahead of yourself and into worrying about something or someone who wasn't even in your life at the moment? Can you determine what triggered it?

It's by habit, generally, that we get into the hoped-for tomorrows of our lives. Am I willing to develop a new habit? That's the primary question. What will I do to facilitate it?

I will take this opportunity before bedtime to think about it and make some notes for myself.

Day 4
Morning

Criticism is never loving.

How many times have we said, "I am just telling you this for your own good"? Truthfully, we know full well it was never a comment for someone else's good. We said it with the intent of undermining our friend or colleague. That's what the ego does with relish. When we are harboring self-doubt, we find solace in creating it in others. How twisted, to think this way and make this choice. The better choice is to say nothing if we can't say something kind.

The quickest remedy for our own self-doubt is to express appreciation for the presence of someone else. It's an interesting by-product, isn't it? Kindness toward others enhances our self-esteem. Who we decide to see "out there" can define who we can become. No exceptions.

I am in the seat of all power today. Who I see is who I am now or who I can become in the next moment.

Day 4
Evening

Did I offer kind comments to all my companions today, or was I critical to someone? If so, it's important for me to discover what prompted my criticism and to make the appropriate amends. Can I see that whatever I say to someone else is really a reflection of how I am feeling about me?

My interactions with others are always a shorthand to who I am in the moment. Before sleeping tonight, I will take the time to replay and then correct in my mind those interactions that should have been different.

Day 5

Morning

We can make a positive difference in the life of everyone we see today. Let's do it.

A wonderful rule of thumb is to ask ourselves, "Is what I am about to do or say going to please God?" And if it isn't (and we always know), pick another response for the situation. If any one of us makes the choice to be kind and loving even once today, it will have an impact that reaches far beyond the moment we're experiencing. The good and the bad ripple outward and onward.

Accepting our role in bettering this world by our individual actions gives every one of us a significant purpose. We never have to wonder what God's will for us might be when we remember this.

I have a very important contribution to make today, and every day. It requires no technical skill, only willingness.

Day 5
Evening

Did I do my part to make this a better world today? Specifically, what did I do? I will make a note of that. I am reminded of my mother's adage when I was a youngster: "If you can't say something nice, say nothing at all." Where might I have behaved better today? Looking at the kinds of responses I made, can I see the work I need to do?

I will ask God to help me be a better person tomorrow. By going to sleep with this prayer in mind, I will receive the guidance I need.

Day 6

Morning

Abuse of any kind is triggered by fear. This is true with no exceptions.

We may think of physical abuse as far worse than verbal abuse, but both reflect the perpetrator's fear. And the effects, though appearing more severe when the abuse is physical, are equally harmful to the psyche of the victim.

Being willing to forgive the person who harmed us in any way seems unfathomable initially, particularly if the abuse was severe. However, our resentment will hold us hostage with as much tenacity as it holds the victimizer. We will never find peace in our own lives as long as we hold another person responsible for our feelings, regardless of how that person interacted with us in the past.

I am the only one who can move my heart to feelings of gladness. Today is the right day to let go of any past hurts.

Day 6
Evening

Did I let resentment fester today? Was it from a recent hurt or one that happened long ago? Taking a moment to journal about it will help me see the folly of hanging on to it. Having a better plan for tomorrow will help me too.

I will seek the help of God, and I will pray for all those people who I am holding resentments against. I know that's the way to find greater peace in my life.

Day 7
Morning

Arguments always take place when one or both parties are afraid.

Every expression, verbal or silent, that anyone makes reflects either love or fear. And both wear many masks. Fear may appear as an argument. It may be a sullen response. Maybe silence. Or perhaps it's an ugly action, or worse, a violent one. It might have occurred randomly, in fact. Or so it seemed.

Many fearful expressions may be so subtle that only one who is privy to the expression recognizes that something sinister lay beneath it.

Love is seldom misunderstood. It might be a simple smile rather than a bouquet of roses, but it's recognizable.

I need to be conscious, always, of how I am about to respond in every situation today. Does it show love or fear? It's never too late to correct it.

Day 7

Evening

Did I get into an argument today? If so, what precipitated it? Do I have amends to make for my part? Taking some time to inventory who I was today will be the best way for me to understand myself. It's also the only way I can be certain of how to correct behavior that's not helpful to others and myself. Here's the place to begin, and now is the time.

I can only be the person my God wants me to be if I know who I am right now.

Week 10
Quiet Your Mind

The constantly chattering mind is so common—and controllable. We surrender to the chatter, generally out of habit (and quite mindlessly in fact), instead of taking control and seeking to empty our minds. But we can learn the process of emptying them, and the meditations here in Week 10 will help.

Perhaps you are wondering why it's important to have an empty mind. The reason is simple: God cannot get our attention if we are consumed by the chatter that fills up our minds' empty spaces. So much of the chatter is nonsensical. Or it's a replay of, "They said, and I should have said." Or it's a soliloquy about how unfair life is.

If our minds aren't quiet and receptive to God's input, we simply cannot fulfill the purpose for which we are here. We must become willing to release the thoughts that clutter our minds.

Day 1

Morning

We can cultivate any thought we want. Some will take root as better life habits than others will.

We must be vigilant about this process of cultivation. It's far too easy to let negative thoughts multiply. And they will, like crabgrass. But healthy thoughts, the ones that shower love and forgiveness on ourselves and others, are as close as our willingness to be quiet so we can hear them. They won't foist themselves on us. We have to make space for them in our minds.

We can look at this process as an adventure. With anticipation, we can observe how our lives change as our thoughts change. And we can see how being quiet really does let God have a chance to move us in the direction that's right for us.

I have a great opportunity today to experiment with this new way of being. Seeking quiet will give me the thoughts that help my life.

Day 1
Evening

How many times today did I have to stop and remember to get quiet?
There is no shame in having to do this. It's a new habit, after all.

I will take some time to write about my experiences with this process.
How did getting quiet feel? How did it change the rest of the day?

I am so thankful there is another way to live my life. Aren't you?

Day 2
Morning

Our thoughts are created by us, protected by us, savored by us. Changing them is up to us too.

We are often in the company of people who express strong opinions. It may not be easy to refrain from being influenced. And if an idea that appeals to us is shared, it's okay to adopt it as one of our own. But letting someone take control of our thinking isn't wise or healthy, nor is it beneficial to the relationship.

One of the greatest gifts we have been given in this life is the ability to choose our thoughts, and there are a multitude of thoughts available to us on every topic. Turning to God, rather than to a fellow traveler, for guidance makes sense. Through His guidance, we can internalize thoughts that are most conducive to a peaceful life.

If I want to maintain a peaceful demeanor today, perhaps it's best to let God help me choose the thoughts I will savor.

Day 2

Evening

What is most obvious about the thoughts I protected today? Can I list the healthy ones as well as the ones that were not helpful? Is there a pattern to my thoughts? A trigger, perhaps, for the ones that aren't helpful?

I could have changed any one of them midstream. If I could think any thought over, what would I change it to?

I will ask God to help me dream only good thoughts tonight. That will help me live only good thoughts tomorrow too.

Day 3
Morning

Choosing another thought, one that's more beneficial to us and others, takes nothing more than willingness and a reliance on God.

Why would we want to choose another thought? Sometimes we don't, in fact. We want to hang on to our anger and our resentments. We feel justified holding others hostage to our unhealthy thoughts. But there is so much more joy available to us if we choose a different perception, one that's in step with God.

Shifting our perception isn't as hard as it may sound, but it can seldom be done alone, at least initially. Asking God to help us makes sense. Next, willingness to get quiet so that G od can reach us with a better thought is necessary. Whatever our inner dialogue is initiates our thoughts. Inviting God into the conversation assures us of having a helpful thought as a choice.

Willingness is my assignment today. If I am not thinking in a way that benefits others or myself, I have the option to seek God's help.

Day 3
Evening

Turning to God for help today was a gift to myself as well as to God. It's great to experience God as a friend who wants to be called upon. What were my opportunities today? Do I see these falling into a particular pattern? Did I experience any miracles today?

Here is a great place to share how successfully I shifted my perception during my experiences with others today. Any success is how a new way of thinking begins. It is the start of a new habit, one that's more beneficial.

I will give myself a pat on the back today for the many times I attempted to shift my perception. And I will thank God for his help too.

Day 4
Morning

We are never at the mercy of a thought or a feeling we don't want.

Empowerment is the gift we experience when we embrace the truth of this idea. It lifts us up, allowing every feeling we have to be shifted. It reminds us of our strength in the face of any thought that blocks our peace of mind. Our partnership with God is enhanced every time we accept this gift.

We deserve to be all-powerful in this one respect, particularly since we are powerless over so much of our life. Other people's ideas and behavior are not ours to control, but our own belong to no one else. If we are not happy with the circumstances of our lives, it's time to look at the thoughts and feelings we are harboring. They can be changed. All else will change too.

I can turn to God whenever the need arises today. If I am not happy with any circumstance, that's the indicator I need.

Day 4
Evening

Did I have a good day today? What thoughts helped and what thoughts hindered my peace of mind? Can I see how turning to God alleviates all my problems?

Writing a short narration of my day, highlighting the times I turned to God and the results I experienced, will help me see how effective this approach is.

I will seek to have an experience with God while sleeping tonight. I will awake well rested.

Day 5

Morning

Our minds contain two voices waiting to be recognized. One is loud. One is gentle. We are the chooser.

It is so much easier to hear the loud voice. It incessantly calls to us, pushing us to criticize others, compare ourselves to others, argue with them, and judge them too. It never shuts up. But behind its call is the other voice. It is ever present, always waiting for us. Are we willing to allow it to be heard?

If we want to hear our inner guide, we must be willing to lay aside our reliance on the louder voice. Its aim is never to help us. On the contrary, its intent is to make us unhappy, fearful, and withdrawn. It doesn't want us to be healed and whole. It wants to keep us stuck and dependent on it. But we can say, "No."

I will choose to hear the quiet voice today and say, "Yes," to it. My day will reflect the voice I hear.

Day 5

Evening

Which voice captured my attention today? How many times did the loud one hold me hostage? There is no shame in that, but it's a good time to journal about the effects of that voice on my life. Can I envision how the day might have gone had I listened to the other one?

I chose what I heard today. I will choose tomorrow too. Does looking at the experiences of today give me food for thought? What might be the better plan for tomorrow?

Day 6
Morning

Life is purposeful for everyone. There are no exceptions. It's not uncommon to fret about what direction we should take in our lives. Few people, if any, are born with a certainty of purpose. Many false starts are common. Relying on our ego for direction, which is our natural inclination, will seldom lead us to the purpose God may have in mind. However, we may learn some lessons that will benefit us anyway.

There is only one way to clearly discern our purpose, and that's in the quiet moments we spend with God. We'll not always be patient enough to wait for the guidance we need. Fortunately, it will wait for us to seek it a second time. God never tires of waiting. And our rightful purpose is unchanging. What joy in being reminded that no one is without purpose.

I am not immaterial to any moment today. I have a voice that needs to be heard, and I have a part to play. Do I know what it is?

Day 6
Evening

Were my actions in sync with God's voice today? Any that weren't can be forgiven as long as I own them. Sharing them will keep me honest.

Looking over the day's activities and the responses I made helps me to see what I need to do. Whether or not I am willing is the question.

If my willingness wavers, I can go to God in prayer before bed tonight. Tomorrow can be a better day.

Day 7

Morning

Being confused about our purpose is natural. Returning to the quiet, again and again, will allow us to feel the direction that is right for us.

Many years ago, at a time when I lived mostly in a state of terror, I read Richard Bach's *Illusions*. On the back cover, I was reminded that if I still lived, I had not yet fulfilled my purpose. This gave me the hope I was not able to muster on my own. God gets our attention in myriad ways. I had finally noticed this book, which had been on my desk for months, and I didn't doubt that the message was coming straight from Him.

In that moment, even though I still wasn't aware of exactly what I needed to do next, I knew that God would tell me. I knew that all was well. I knew that I had an inner guide who was in charge. And I unquestioningly knew that just being quiet was my part of the equation.

I will trust in the plan for me today. It's right. And if I can't hear what it is, I will just be kind.

Day 7

Evening

What an exciting awareness I had today. Right? Did I detect my purpose? Was I listening for it? Recounting the activities of the day, where is the evidence I understood God's plan for me? Were there times I felt confused? What did I do then? Can I see my role and God's role? How do they differ?

I can be grateful for any awareness I had today. I will thank God before sleep comes for helping me be open to His voice.

Week 11

Every Encounter Is a Holy Encounter– Respond Accordingly

Since my introduction to this idea from *A Course in Miracles* decades ago, I have savored it. I have not always remembered it when in discussions with others, but I have come to appreciate that remembering it even occasionally has an important impact on my experiences with all people.

No one comes into our lives accidentally. Every person we encounter is necessary to our personal journey, and we are participants in holy, sacred conversations every moment of the day. We don't have to understand this for it to be true. And we likely won't remember it much of the time—we seldom live that consciously every minute. But that doesn't change what's true.

We are on a holy journey. Pleasing God by our actions is the assignment throughout Week 11. Everywhere we look, a holy encounter is calling to us.

Day 1

Morning

Every time we choose to see our companions as separate, we complicate our journey.

The habit of judging our companions is well rooted in our psyches. We feel disconnected from God, and this awful sense of separation creates the fear that leads naturally to our judgment of others, which then results in even deeper feelings of separation.

We get caught in a vicious maelstrom that can only be healed by having a shift in perception. We must be willing to entertain this shift, and if we are, we will see our companions as our holy teachers, chosen by us for the lessons we have come here to learn.

I have the opportunity to see my companions as my teachers today, holy in every instance. Will I take that opportunity?

Day 1
Evening

How aware was I of my many "teachers" today? Did I gratefully acknowledge their holy presence by absorbing their contributions to my journey? I will take this opportunity to list them by name and contribution. I want to see the pattern of my life and how it is unfolding. I can best do this by recounting all of the experiences I had today.

I will sleep well tonight if I first say "Thank you" to each of my teachers and to God.

Day 2
Morning

We will always respond appropriately to our companions if we speak from our hearts, saying what God would want us to say.

God's perspective on every one of us is loving. Seeking to share that perspective, to see Spirit in everyone, takes little more than willingness. We'll never harm others if we let God's vision serve as our eyes. We'll never disrupt anyone's journey if we speak only the words God would say. We'll reach our own final destination with joy in our hearts if we have done our work here well.

Our purpose is simple: Be kind. It's to see God in everyone. It's to recognize that when others are not kind, they are afraid and need an extra measure of kindness from us. It's to know that God has orchestrated the whole of our lives and we can rest easily, knowing our journey is part of the grand plan.

Today will be as quietly peaceful as I want it to be. My work is to see my companions as my loving teachers.

Day 2

Evening

Speaking from my heart is easier in some instances than others. Listing the easy experiences first will help me be honest about the whole day. How did I feel when I let my heart guide my words and actions? Can I relate to how my companions responded? When I chose another way to interact, what happened? Did I feel differently? How did my companions respond?

The point in all of this is for me to see that who I bring to the table determines who joins me there. What did I learn today?

Before going to sleep, I need to prepare my mind for making any amends that might be necessary as the result of today's interactions. God will help me.

Day 3
Morning

Seek to see the good and be grateful for it. It's the best choice to make in every experience.

Looking for the good in every moment is a great adventure. It allows us to anticipate joyfully what is just around the corner. If we believe that God is always present in each moment and that every experience is designed to help fulfill our purpose, we won't harbor dread or experience any fear as we walk toward it. We are not journeying alone. Ever.

There is a schedule to the events in our lives. No experience is haphazardly coming. No person is present without reason. Every breath we take is holy, and it's the lifeline to the specific encounters that are waiting for our acknowledgment and acceptance. We can cherish this information, or we can resist it. But what we need to learn will wait.

I am here now to fulfill God's will with these people and these experiences.

Day 3

Evening

How frequently did I see the blessing in the events of my life today? Can I see that even when I didn't like the experience, it was a blessing? How could I tell? What was the biggest lesson today? What would I most like to thank others for today? I will make a list of those blessings and acknowledge those people tomorrow who helped me grow today.

I can go to sleep grateful tonight knowing that I am exactly where I need to be, on a journey that wears my name.

Day 4
Morning

We are on a mutually complementary journey with our companions.

It's with intent that our paths intersect. We often forget this, and then we harbor fear instead of looking for the lesson and the good that's ever-present. Some even believe we made a pact with one another before coming into this life we are sharing, a pact to teach and learn from each other. This idea may not resonate with some of us, but choosing to dispense with our disbelief for a while does help clarify our experiences.

The one idea we can all embrace is that God accompanies us on this journey. He is present for every conversation; He is part of every activity; He orchestrates our hopes and dreams. Deciding to remember this can change how every minute of today will look.

I am eager to see what will come my way today. It will be part of the divine plan I am ready for.

Day 4
Evening

Was I able to see how my companions were complementing my journey today? Journaling about the day's activities, the people I spent time with, and the apparent lessons offered to me will help me realize the intent and the value of all that happens, not just today but every day.

I am so glad to be reminded that there are no superfluous experiences in my life. I will gladly remember this as I prepare to go to sleep tonight.

Day 5
Morning

God always knows what we need. Believing this takes the distaste out of the experiences we don't like.

No one says we have to like every experience that calls to us. But God will never lead us into a relationship or an experience that will harm us. What we have to guard against, however, is the tendency to let the ego make a choice for us and claim that it's God's will when it clearly isn't. How will we know? In the quiet space of our mind, it's self-evident.

It's comforting to embrace the knowledge that God is in charge of our learning curve. It makes more palatable the many experiences that don't appeal to us but stretch us just the same. We are never really confused about this, only resistant. The ego prefers being in charge of the learning curve.

I will look to this day with glad anticipation and remember that God is sending me what I need.

Day 5

Evening

What did God send me today? Do I know? Am I grateful? Writing about it is an excellent exercise. I need to acknowledge the gifts I received. How did my ego interfere today? Did I succumb to its wishes? How did that make me feel? Journaling about that too will help me make better choices tomorrow.

I thank you, God, for helping me see the real gifts that were present today.

Day 6
Morning

Making a detailed gratitude list is the surest way to cure whatever seems to be troubling us.

We get stuck in "stinking thinking" so easily. That's the nature of being human. The pity pot is an easy place to plop whenever we aren't getting our way. Instead of considering that God might have a plan for us that's better than our best thinking, we pout, certain that we deserve something better (or at least different).

When this is our mindset, perhaps it's time to count our blessings. Let's make a list of the many wonderful people with which we are sharing this moment in time. Let's also note the many experiences that have helped us grow. We may not have liked all of them, in the midst of them, but we can see their value now. Can't we?

I will try to be aware of the goodies coming my way as they present themselves today.

Day 6

Evening

Doing a gratitude list is affirming. It makes me aware of God's presence in the many details of my life. Doing one every time I am in a funk is a great exercise, and one I will begin tonight before going to bed.

Perhaps reading old lists will be valuable too. Tonight, I will create a folder, title it "I Am Grateful For," and put all of the lists in one place so that I can get the accumulative effect as the days and months pass.

I am making great progress in changing my life by changing how I am thinking. How good this feels.

Day 7

Morning

We cannot heal whatever troubles our hearts or minds in isolation.

If ever we wonder why a certain person continues to appear in our lives, it's because we have work to do with that person. In our relationships with others—those we consider friends and loved ones and those who may be less easily appreciated—we are constantly being presented with the opportunities we need for our growth and theirs.

Nothing happens coincidentally. That's the comforting realization, if we can wrap our minds around it. It makes all of the experiences that felt difficult in the past more acceptable to us now. We all need one another. We cannot heal our hearts or minds if we don't do the work that's required. The time is now.

I will go into this day hopeful and full of acceptance. What comes to me comes with the blessing of God.

Day 7

Evening

Did I welcome my many companions into the experiences we shared today? Writing a description of those good experiences will keep me mindful of my part in successful encounters. Practicing the good eliminates the bad.

Were there any I resisted? Can I talk about them with someone? Figuring out why I resisted is the lesson I need to learn. Am I willing? With God's help, I can change any part of my behavior.

Being grateful for the successes and thanking God will help me have more of them tomorrow.

Week 12

Choose the Quiet Voice of Loving-Kindness

Two voices are vying for our attention, always. One voice is always loud, argumentative, and bent on controlling others, a stance that usually creates disharmony.

The other voice is soft and compels us to express only loving-kindness to all of the people we meet throughout the day. We live in a state of peace and harmony when we listen to this voice. But to hear it, we must listen closely.

We are constantly making the choice of which one to hear. Why we would ever choose the one that makes us uneasy and resentful is mysterious, but that's the power of the ego. It wants us to think we are always right, at any cost. When we listen to it, we stray from peace. But when we listen to the other, softer voice, we eliminate disharmony. I have the freedom to choose what I hear. How hard can it really be to make the wiser choice? Week 12 will emphasize this principle.

Day 1
Morning

One voice is our friend, the other one is not. Both will call to us today.

Our vulnerability often determines which voice we succumb to. If we are not feeling confident and connected to God and the other people sharing our path, we are prone to listen to the ego, which then exaggerates our feelings of separation. This makes our fellow travelers seem like enemies to be feared, and it makes listening to the quieter voice nearly impossible.

There is a way out of this conundrum, though. We can sit quietly for a moment, take a few deep breaths, and envision God's Spirit waiting quietly for our attention. The minute we give it to God rather than the ego, a shift in our experience happens. How lucky we are to have this gift of being able to change our perspective.

I may need to shift my perspective in some situation today. But I can do it. It takes only a moment.

Day 1

Evening

How many times did I listen to my ego today? What was the result of paying attention to that voice? Can I see where making that choice complicated my relationships? Writing about those experiences will help me make the better choice tomorrow.

What evidence do I have that the Holy Spirit guided some of my actions today? Can I see the payoff of adhering to the Spirit's voice?

I will replay in my mind some of the peaceful experiences I had today. They will help me sleep comfortably.

Day 2
Morning

Every loving thought is true. Everything else is an appeal for healing and help, regardless of the form it takes.

This idea is a wonderful bit of shorthand regarding our interactions with others. If what we are experiencing from others in these interactions isn't loving, someone's ego must be holding sway, and we can remember that an appeal for help and healing is being made.

Offering love in those instances changes the one who is hurting, the experience, and us too.

The ego can be ignored—not easily though. But practice helps. The peaceful presence of the Holy Spirit is always there, and when we want a gentle experience, we must turn to it. We can probably assume that many of the experiences we are invited to will make listening to our ego quite attractive. Fortunately, we can resist. That's the opportunity and the lesson that's always being held out to us.

I will be pulled in two directions today. One comes from my ego. The other comes from the Holy Spirit. Which one will claim me?

Day 2
Evening

How many loving thoughts did I hear or see expressed from others today? Listing them will make me more aware of them in the future. How many times did I counter someone's angry ego with a loving response? I will list those instances too. It's important for me to be cognizant of all my interactions and choices. They won't all be peaceful, but I can learn from all of them anyway.

Am I ending my day feeling pretty good about how I interacted with my fellow travelers today? What's the main thing I will practice tomorrow?

Day 3
Morning

Choosing to be peaceful rather than right is an excellent solution to any conflict.

Needing to be right is a mindset many of us fall into. Perhaps that's what we observed happening in our family of origin, so we were imprinted with this pattern of behavior from infancy. But it's not the only way to function in our relationships with others. In fact, it destroys relationships quite readily.

Some may think that not sticking up for an opinion means you'll be perceived as weak or unworthy of being heard. It's never wrong to express an opinion, and if others choose to adopt it, great. But being opinionated to the point of real conflict isn't ever productive. It's in these exchanges that the one willing to choose peace rather than continue the argument nurtures the only solution that's sensible.

Will I be willing to be the one seeking peace today?

Day 3
Evening

Did I add to the mix of conflict today or did I seek peace? This is a good time to write about the ups and downs of the day. I surely had some successes. What were they? Where might I have done a better job of interacting with others? Can I see where the work remains?

I will ask God in prayer to help me be willing to do my work. I can begin as I fall asleep, in fact.

Day 4

Morning

Each peaceful choice contributes to world peace too. Perhaps this idea seems a bit too lofty; however, why not trust it enough to give it a try? It feels good to interact peacefully with our contemporaries, whomever they are. Being in conflict with anyone doesn't feel good. Even people who claim to love a good argument don't rest easily until the dust settles. And that generally happens when one person decides to seek peace instead.

Being the one to seek peace is a very worthy choice for many reasons. It lowers blood pressure, lessens aches and pains, and suppresses anxiety. Everyone benefits when peace is sought—those close by and those very far away.

I will do my part for peace today.

Day 4
Evening

How successfully did I negotiate my many encounters today? Was I frequently a proponent for peace? Listing the times I responded peacefully rather than escalating an argument will help me remember that making another choice is always possible.

Did I ever force a disagreement today? Can I look back on it now and see how another choice would have been wiser? What's the main thing I learned in today's experiences?

Am I headed to bed willing to take responsibility for the times I didn't add peace to a situation? Have I made a better plan for tomorrow?

Day 5
Morning

Willingness is what allows us to change our minds.

We don't have to be held hostage by our old ideas just because they have been with us for a long time. Being flexible and open to new information is a sign of growth and spiritual maturity. But the resistance to change can be overwhelming. That's why willingness is a good first step. It can best be acquired through prayer. The God of our understanding is always close at hand.

Getting free from an old idea, particularly one that has begun to cripple us, is what our journey is about. We are here to learn a multitude of lessons, and we have to make room for new ones by letting go of those we have outgrown. Our work is never done as long as we are alive. Our purpose continues to unfold. With willingness, we can see the excitement in this.

Freedom from an old idea is my choice today. My first step will be willingness. Then comes joy.

Day 5

Evening

Was I stuck in an old idea today? Did that prevent me from being a good listener or from growing as the result of some new information? If I can say "Yes" to these questions, I need to revisit the day's experiences in my mind and reframe what could have been different. I will write the preferred scenario. For instance, what might I have said and then what might have happened?

Replaying in my mind the better way to show up in situations is good practice. I will do this as I prepare to go to sleep.

Day 6
Morning

Just for today, I can do one thing that benefits all of humankind.

The joy of realizing we have only this day, these twenty-four hours, to concern ourselves with makes everything manageable, doesn't it? No longer do we need to wonder what might come next week or next year. There is only now. And in this moment, we can be kind. We can spread a bit of joy around. We can trust that God will help us do whatever is ours to do. There is no mystery to living in the present. There is only relief.

Being willing to express the hope, joy, and kindness that we are so freely given by the God of our understanding is the only work we have to do on this day that stands before us. It's the very work that is expected of all of us. Am I willing to do my part?

I am where I need to be right now. God is here with me, prompting me about what I need to do next. Am I listening?

Day 6
Evening

The joy of having only these twenty-four hours to attend to is delicious. I didn't always appreciate this, however. I used to spin into the future too easily. What's the evidence that I stuck with this day only, today?

Do I have examples of the old me too? When I worried about what might or might not happen? There's no shame in that, of course. Only wasted energy and lack of trust. How might today have been better? Writing some examples will help me not to repeat them.

I'm making progress. I can see it. And I am grateful.

Day 7
Morning

There is no timetable for changing our lives. When, or if, we do it is our choice.

It's a relief to know that we can choose how we will respond to any situation that bids for our attention. One of the easiest choices we can make is to say nothing if we are being invited to a conflict. Another easy choice is to ask God to help us see any confusing or difficult situation from another perspective. And then there's being willing to see that anyone's attack on us is a mark of that person's fear. It's not about us, and we don't have to respond accordingly.

Our lives can be simpler than we make them. By making the choice to change our responses to myriad experiences, by seeing we need not be fearful but rather can be filled with love, we will discover a peace that we had not known was possible. That's our opportunity. Right now. Today.

I will have the life I deserve if I make loving choices today.

Day 7

Evening

How peaceful was today? Do I know what I could have done differently? Will I be willing the next time? I will replay the day as it could have been, including the responses I might have chosen. Then I will look back on it and smile. I can be all that I really want to be.

With God's help, which is always here, I will find joy in my dreams and in my life tomorrow.

Closing Thoughts

The twelve-week program has come to a close. Do you think it has moved you along the path to a more peaceful life? I hope the answer is "Yes."

I also hope you increased your understanding that every experience along the way is intentional and full of promise for your purpose in this life. I hope you grew accustomed to recognizing that anyone's attack on you was actually that person's call for healing and help, and thus your opportunity to express only love.

Coming to appreciate and understand every experience with any one of the many companions on your journey—those you see daily and those who simply, almost imperceptibly pass through your life—clears away the confusion you so frequently feel, doesn't it?

If there are some principles that continue to be difficult, you can always return to them for another week of practice. This is a lifelong journey. That's the good news! It's progress we're after, not perfection. And you made progress, I am sure of that. No one who applies themselves to this simple program will escape some growth.

I know you learned the value of shifting your perspective (that is, seeking to see a situation from another angle). Perhaps you don't do it successfully at every opportunity, but even once a day offers a payoff. I know it feels better to give up the judgments that are so easily made against others. Learning that your judgments actually reveal how you feel about *yourself* is valuable information. Being reminded to let go of outcomes is a simple suggestion and it offers such relief. Not doing for others what they need to do for themselves gives you the freedom you need to attend to your own journey while allowing your contemporaries the freedom they need to live their own lives too. No one benefits when you mind someone else's business.

Being able to celebrate that you aren't in control of anything but yourself, your own attitude, and your own opinions and behavior takes willingness. But once you have experienced the freedom that comes with giving up control of the uncontrollable, you'll never want to return to your former obsession as a daily way of life.

Perhaps best of all, coming to appreciate that you are constantly choosing which voice to listen to means you can always choose the quieter, more loving, peaceful voice. This ensures that you will not harm others. Ever. You will recognize the holiness of the many people who travel with you. Listening intently to that voice means you will be carrying the message that God has called you here to carry. That's the primary lesson for you, and for me too.

Thanks for taking this journey with me. May the peace of your present carry you confidently into your future.

About the Author

Karen Casey, winner of a 2007 Johnson Institute America Honors Recovery Award for her contributions to the field, is a sought-after speaker at recovery and spirituality conferences throughout the country. She has written thirty-one books, among them *Peace a Day At a Time, 52 Ways to Live the Course in Miracles, 20 Things I Know For Sure, Codependence and the Power of Detachment,* and *Change Your Mind and Your Life Will Follow*—a bestselling book that is the basis for her Change Your Mind Workshops—plus many more. Her renowned bestseller *Each Day a New Beginning: Daily Meditations for Women,* originally published in 1982, has sold more than 4 million copies and been translated into ten different languages.

Karen Casey divides her time between Minnesota and Florida. To learn more about her work , visit her at www.womens-spirituality. com or at her Facebook page: Karen Casey, Author

Mango Publishing, established in 2014, publishes an eclectic list of books by diverse authors—both new and established voices—on topics ranging from business, personal growth, women's empowerment, LGBTQ+ studies, health, and spirituality to history, popular culture, time management, decluttering, lifestyle, mental wellness, aging, and sustainable living. We were named 2019 *and* 2020's #1 fastest-growing independent publisher by *Publishers Weekly*. Our success is driven by our main goal, which is to publish high-quality books that will entertain readers as well as make a positive difference in their lives.

Our readers are our most important resource; we value your input, suggestions, and ideas. We'd love to hear from you—after all, we are publishing books for you!

Please stay in touch with us and follow us at:

Facebook: Mango Publishing
Twitter: @MangoPublishing
Instagram: @MangoPublishing
LinkedIn: Mango Publishing
Pinterest: Mango Publishing
Newsletter: mangopublishinggroup.com/newsletter

Join us on Mango's journey to reinvent publishing, one book at a time.